Infinite Possibilities

How Finding Love Online Can Work For You Too!

Hyleath Rose

iUniverse, Inc.
New York Bloomington

INFINITE POSSIBILITIES
How Finding Love Online Can Work For You Too!

iUniverse books may be ordered through booksellers or by contacting:

*iUniverse
1663 Liberty Drive
Bloomington, IN 47403
www.iuniverse.com
1-800-Authors (1-800-288-4677)*

ISBN: 978-1-4502-1452-0 (sc)
ISBN: 978-1-4502-1453-7 (e-book)

Printed in the United States of America

iUniverse rev. date: 3/15/2010

Contents

Acknowledgements

First and foremost I would like to thank God for blessing me with the talent to write, the drive to succeed and the wisdom to ask for help when I needed it the most. To everyone who has supported me in all my goals and dreams, you will always hold a special place in my heart. A very special thank you goes out to Katrina Jones, my number one supporter and close friend. Without her none of this would be possible.

Introduction

I found myself lost in our conversations for the past six months. The restaurant he chose has a delectable menu of selections and he suggests a dish that he thinks I may like. As I stare into his eyes from across the table, I almost pinch myself to see if I'm actually dreaming. His face is so handsome and his smile lights up the room. Our goals and aspirations are in sync and I almost feel like I met the missing piece to my life's puzzle. A life no longer spent watching T.V. or curled up alone with a book. I've read countless romance novels that describe this feeling, but I never imagined I would experience the same feeling for myself. I was initially disheartened by the process because my first six dates were unsuccessful, but I suppose seven really is my lucky number. I was so close to deleting my profile, but now I'm thankful I changed my mind. Having been single for the past six years I accepted the reality that a partner would not be a part of my future. Taking a risk and putting my profile out there took me off the couch and plunged me into a whole new dating world. It opened up a world of people I never knew existed. People I'm sure I would never have encountered any other way, but for the Internet. It all started with an overheard conversation about how thankful they were for the Internet. Little did that happy couple know that their blossoming romance was going to change my life forever. Initially I was unsure of the possibilities for me because I had so many prior dating disappointments. I finally asked the question why not me? The answer to my question is sitting across from me now and I'm satisfied with the results. Never in a million years did I think all of this would have started with an email that said: "I read your profile and I'm very interested in getting to know more about you."

Who ever imagined the Internet would become a popular place to meet the potential love of your life? Overnight, the Internet transformed into a virtual single's bar without the smoke, alcohol or cover charge. Attractive, average, funny, non-smoker, conversationalist are all words people use to describe themselves in their Internet personal ads. Those words are designed to make someone appear more attractive to you. Yes you the single woman! Newly divorced, coming out of a long term relationship, sick of the options in your present dating pool, or haven't really dated much are all reasons you should give the Internet a try. Men are looking for women of all shapes, sizes, races and personalities. Some men desire marriage, others an activity partner or just good old fashioned friendship. The Internet is widely used now to find whatever you're looking for in a partner. Society leads us to believe that every woman desires to be married. That is not always the case. If you want to casually date, an activity partner or simply want to meet new people, the Internet can open those doors for you. I'm not suggesting that you can't find what you're looking for in your random day to day life. I'm suggesting that your odds will increase dramatically when you incorporate the Internet into your dating options. Using the Internet to meet people is very common for some women, yet others are still skeptical of the concept of meeting someone using a computer. The same people you meet on the Internet are the same people you could meet on the street. On numerous occasions, I've run into people whose profiles I've seen online at the grocery store, gym, and even at work.

The benefits of choosing to date online are:

1) **When you're on a dating website you know the men are there for similar reasons.**

Anyone who chooses to display themselves publicly on a dating website is looking for something. You just need to find the one looking for the same thing you are.

2) You can remain within your comfort level without any pressure.

There are several methods of approaching on-line dating. Which ever method you prefer is entirely up to you. No pressure.

3) You can screen potentials without the hassle of interacting with them.

You decide who you would like to converse with by responding to an email or not responding. If you're not interested no explanation is necessary.

You would be surprised how many men are looking for someone just like you, but they experience the same difficulties you do.

Meeting People Randomly Can Be Difficult.

The success of a chance encounter hinges on several factors. First of all, it takes a lot of nerve and courage on someone's part to show interest. Many times I've noticed a guy I was attracted to and allowed the opportunity to pass me by without saying something to him. How do I show him I'm interested? If I say something and get rejected how will I pick my ego up off the ground? I used excuses for not expressing my interest. He may think

I'm too desperate if I make the first move. He probably already has someone in his life. He's probably not even interested in me. If he were interested enough, then he would approach me and try to strike up a conversation. Any number of those excuses could have been valid or invalid, but only a psychic knows what's really going through a man's minds. The potential for rejection kept me from expressing my interest, and those men may have used my same rationale for not making an introduction.

One day while walking my dog in my neighborhood, I noticed a guy walking down my street. On this particular day I was in a good mood and said "hello" while thinking nothing of the gesture. My gesture presented him with an opening to speak to me. Unbeknownst to me, he noticed me on several other occasions and was interested in getting to know me better. Without my prompting, he would have never had the nerve to approach me. I created an opening when I said "hello." We actually dated for about a year after meeting. My decision to say "hello" was a random occurrence that day. The success of chance encounters has a lot to do with being in the right place at the right time and under the right circumstances. A lot of women are under the misguided impression that a man will pursue them if they're interested. I've had conversations with numerous men who fear rejection. Their fear prevents them from approaching women they're attracted to.

For example, have you ever been in the grocery store and you can feel a man watching you. You can tell by his constant stares that he wants to say something to you, but he never does. If you met under different social circumstances perhaps an opportunity to speak would occur with less pressure. Some men handle a woman's disinterest easily, while others refuse to even take the chance. The possibility of a connection is surpassed by the potential blow to their egos. The Internet relieves that tension for both of you. It gives the users a medium to put themselves out there without any public embarrassment. If you find someone of interest online there is less anxiety to express your interest.

If The Object Of Your Affections Doesn't Share The Same Interest, There's No Harm Done And It's Effortless To Move On.

Finding the person for you online may come easily. It also might take a while. That's the area I'm going to explore; finding what you're looking for with the click of a mouse. At the onset of the Internet, there were only a handful of websites designed for matchmaking. Now, the web is inundated with a variety of websites for every dater's discriminating taste. Some websites have personality questionnaires allowing them to select potential partners for you, yet others are less sophisticated and simply rely on good old-fashioned laws of attraction.

Do You Prefer The Chase Or To Be Chased?

A lot of Internet dating sites allow you to search their database for free; however if you want to contact someone that generally requires a fee. For the budget-friendly dater, there are still a few free sites available.

Before the Internet

When I was in college and in between boyfriends, I remember receiving an advertisement in the mail about a dating service. The concept piqued my curiosity so I gave them a call. The dating service's sales person wanted a considerable amount of money to set me up on ten dates. At the time I didn't have a lot of money just lying around, nor was I willing to pay them to set up ten possible matches. They also wouldn't offer any guarantees for my financial investment. I may have been persuaded if they'd offered a money back guarantee if they couldn't find me a match. That certainly wouldn't have been a cost effective business plan; however it would have given me some dating peace of mind. The sales person made the concept sound so tempting, but after hanging up with them tons of negative thoughts raced through my mind. What if they didn't have anyone I was attracted to? What if they weren't attracted to me? What if they had a lot of issues? They also required you to visit their offices, fill out paper work, and create a video, all of which seemed too laborious for my taste. Over the years I've actually met a handful of people whom met their mates through dating services or the personal ads. When I was in college, dating phone services were also widespread. They used the conference call concept to connect people. The main thing I didn't like about those services was they didn't seem any different than a blind date. Once, a friend of mine set me up with one of her friends. I knew nothing more about him than what he could have potentially placed in the local personals. When we met I was not attracted to him and his personality was unimpressive. I was very upset that my friend would even put me in that position.

The Internet alleviates a lot of those blind date anxieties. I can determine whether I'm attracted by simply exchanging pictures. I can converse with someone at my own speed via email, IM (instant message) or the telephone. This format for getting to know someone will allow you to decide whether you have genuine interest in someone before planning to meet them. These are all pluses that didn't exist during the newspaper ad era. Additionally, if I'm not interested all I have to do is press delete.

The New Age Of Dating

Everything began for me in 1994. I'd heard of the Internet but never inquired any further. The depth of my computer knowledge was limited to basic word-processing and email. In fact, I was still actually using a word-processor to type my papers. A few short years later I was introduced to the Internet and that introduction significantly changed my dating life. When I was contacted by the matchmaking service, I couldn't fathom spending hundreds of dollars to only be introduced to ten people, but I found out Internet dating was fairly inexpensive and the pool of potentials was much greater. Some of the site's fees can be as cheap as treating yourself out to dinner or buying that cute new pair of shoes. Inevitably you will find that those shoes can't keep you warm at night (unless they're Uggs), and they can't share in pleasant conversation over a nice cozy meal.

Meeting Someone New Always Seems So Complicated.

Internet dating will change your life. You will no longer be reduced to making trips to the grocery store to scope out bachelors only buying chips and TV dinners. You won't have to sit at home wishing someone; anyone would pay attention to you. You won't have to listen to your friends ramble on and on about their extensive dating lives because it seems so effortless for them to meet people. You won't have to hear about them just happening to be in the right place at the right time ALL THE TIME!

Your fingers can do the searching for you in the comfort of your own home. With no makeup on, your hair a mess, wearing your pajamas you can look for a new man like looking for a new pair of shoes.

Unfortunately Human Beings Can Be A Harder Fit Than Those Size Eight Open Toe Wedges.

After graduating from college I wanted to break away from my core friend base and meet some new people. I found the Internet was a great way to do that. I never considered myself a particularly attractive woman as I was very overweight when I began my Internet dating journey. Before the Internet I dated men I met through friends or chance encounters. Some experiences were good and some were bad. Once I joined the online dating game I found out just how many men were actually attracted to me. I had no idea that many options existed for me. My world of dating was very small before the Internet. Since creating my first Internet dating profile, I've easily gone on over one hundred dates. Some have labeled me a serial dater; however that label doesn't bother me because I enjoy going out and meeting new people. Whether it turns out good or bad I'm indifferent. I'm not in the business of wasting anyone's time particularly mine. When I meet someone and I see potential dating red flags, I'm out of there. I've gained lifelong friendships and had several relationships from my Internet experience. I met a man I dated for several years that I met online. When that relationship ended I went back to where it all began. I must say I enjoy having the option of infinite possibilities. I enjoy getting to know new people and getting dressed on a Friday night for a date.

It Beats Sitting At Home Watching T.V.

I've persuaded several of my friends to Internet date after hearing their numerous complaints of solitary living. I've heard countless dating stories and I've also shared my online dating experiences. Those experiences helped me establish my list of Internet dating dos and don'ts. My dating trials and tribulations and process of elimination are the basis of this book. This guide will help you stay safe and avoid the usual traps women fall into when dealing with men we're interested in. When I meet people new to this form of dating I call them "Internet Virgins". Once I relay my years of Internet dating experience they inevitably have a lot of questions regarding the process. The number one question is always, why is this form of dating useful? The answer is simple; it opens up your world to infinite dating possibilities. I have several friends whom live vicariously through my dating life. They always want to hear my personal dating experiences. For some strange reason, women always want to hear the good the bad and the ugly side of being single. When someone asks me if I have any new stories to tell, my normal response is "of course I do, I meet new guys all the time because the Internet provides an endless supply of men." After sharing one of my latest stories, and sharing a laugh or two, a friend of mine suggested that I write a book. She knows a lot of women who needed the extra push to get out of their lonely girl rut.

If Internet Dating Guidelines Existed When I Initially Got Online, I Could Have Avoided A Lot Of Rookie Mistakes.

Even though a lot of commercials make Internet dating appear simple, there can be many pitfalls and major nuances you need to watch out for to avoid any unnecessary dilemmas. The commercials never explain how to deal with rejection. Additionally, they never express the importance of putting yourself out there and sharing your photo on a profile. The commercials don't teach you how to be safe from predators, or how to keep a man's interest once you meet. They don't show you how to determine if a man is interested or wasting your time, and all the dating mistakes women make everyday are void from the commercials. Sometimes it can be as easy as logging on and Mr. Right is presented instantly. The Internet doesn't take away all the issues that can go along with dating.

The Internet Helps You Put Yourself In The Dating Game.

The beauty of this form of dating is that it can be at your own personal speed. You can put one toe in the pond or you can jump right in feet first. Everything you do in this arena is at your own comfort level. You can be a more casual user and create a profile and see who responds, or more aggressive by sending emails to men you're interested in. If you're not interested in someone that contacts you, it's easy to press the delete button. The Internet opens the doors to countless men who may be interested in you. The key is to make yourself available to potential suitors and keep yourself safe and confident in the process.

When I Started Dating Online I Had No Concept Of The Dangers.

Thankfully I was never injured or put in any compromising positions as a result of my naiveté. I thank God for that because I was unbearably naïve. The media has done a great job of informing the public of the dangers of corresponding with strangers. Now we are more aware of all those dangers. The Internet is no place for children to surf without adult supervision and monitoring. Children can be easily manipulated by others. This can make the Internet a dangerous place for immature minds. With all the press of serial killers and child molesters searching the net for their next victim, you have to be smart when dealing with perfect strangers. Even though you believe you have tons of information about an individual and photos, don't trust someone you have never met. A predator will tell you everything you want to hear on the other end of a computer just to keep you captivated. I know these potential dangers are a reason some have chosen to avoid Internet dating. The reality is that these dangers still exist without the use of a computer. When meeting someone new you should be cautious regardless whether you meet them on your computer or at your gym. I know women who have met a man at a club, talked to them on the phone, and then gave him their address to their home to pick them up for a date. They know nothing about this person. We should be cautious when it comes to meeting people online, but we should also have the same caution when meeting anyone new.

My purpose is to help you achieve your dating goals using your computer as the tool. Whether you want a date card filled for every weekend, a long term relationship, casual sex, or an extra-marital relationship this guide will show you the way. Additionally, you will learn how to deal with men and boost your self esteem.

Confidence Is A Major Turn On For Men And It Has Nothing To Do With How You Look. Attraction Is Relative.

You will never know who is or isn't attracted to you, but if you lack self-confidence it can hinder your dating life. When I was younger I shied away from men that I felt were out of my league. Having low self esteem I was shocked at the handsome professional men that were interested in me online. I recognized that I can't say what one man is or is not attracted to. I know a woman who started a website for BBW's (Big Beautiful Women). It was surprising how many men were attracted to women on her website. Now there are several websites that cater to men and women who desire full-figured mates. There are all kinds of websites looking for people with similar interests, attractions and situations. For example there is a dating website for people who have sexually transmitted diseases. This might seem strange for some, but for those suffering from an STD the ability to meet people like themselves is priceless.

This Guide Will Instruct You How To Avoid The Common Pitfalls Of Online Dating.

How do you use the Internet to find out more information on the man you're dating? How do you open up your date card to end your lonely nights at home? How do you gain confidence in yourself and learn how to deal with men on your terms? I can't guarantee that you'll meet your soul mate; however, you're dating life will change dramatically. If you're anything like myself, I used to go from home, to work, to the gym, and out with my friends on occasion. I never met anyone new in my day to day travels. The Internet opened the flood gates to possibilities. That is my promise to you infinite possibilities.

Internet Dating Stigmas

The following are common stigmas attached to Internet dating that deter people from trying it:

1) **You're desperate and can't meet men any other way.**

   This is the new age of dating and meeting people. There is no shame or desperation surrounding using alternative means to find the right person for you.

2) **Its dangerous.**

   There are obvious dangers online. You need to be vigilant and protect yourself at all times;

however it's no different than meeting any new person. I have met people online that I have run into at the gym, grocery store, or out with the girls. The same people you meet online you can meet in the street.

3) You're too old.

I met a woman in her sixties retired in Florida living out her retirement years in the sun. She was a long time divorcee and found a fellow retiree on a dating websites free month trial. She met a man who also was using the free month trial. They exchanged emails for weeks on his last day of the trial he gave her his phone number. They eventually married. There are people of all ages online. There are sites devoted to people of certain ages.

4) I've been single too long. I can't do this.

It's hard for people who have been single for long periods of time or never really had a lot of dating experience, to believe online dating could work for them. I totally disagree. The Internet opens the world. There are men online just like you, who have experienced similar situations and circumstances. Not every man in the world has had worlds of dating experiences. Being divorced and having a hard time getting back on the saddle of dating can apply to both genders. The Internet is a place to connect with him. You could be missing out.

5) What will my friends and family think?

I know a few couples that hide the fact they met online. I also know those whom boast about it. It is entirely your discretion what you choose to reveal to family and friends. Every time I meet someone new, the inevitable question arises "So how did you meet." My general response is "through a friend." They don't have to know my computer is my friend, that's just my little secret.

Do not let any of these reasons deter or prevent you from meeting the love of your life, or at least a date to your office holiday party.

My First Experience

My first Internet dating experience occurred in 1996 during my junior year in college. I was an Accounting major, and knew zilch about computers. We were required to take one or two classes on computers but only as it related to accounting principles. My aunt Olivia had purchased a computer and had an AOL membership. She talked nonstop about all the new things she found online. The men were her biggest topic of conversation. Aunt Olivia was meeting tons of men online. I had to investigate the phenomena, so I immediately went to her house to see what all the fuss was about. I signed onto her computer, she gave me a brief AOL tutorial, and within twenty minutes I was chatting with four men at once on instant message (IM for short). Instant messaging allows you talk to people in real time by typing messages back and forth to each other. Yahoo, AOL and MSN will let you download and use their instant message services for free. I advise anyone attempting to begin online dating to use an IM service. My first experience with instant message was amazing. I've never had that many men paying attention to me at the same time before. They all seemed interested in getting to know more about me. I was amazed by the interest coming from little boxes that were popping up on the computer screen. I came from the school of thought that you meet one man and focused all of your attention on him until you broke up. You were depressed, you cried your eyes out, and then you got over the hurt and waited for the next guy to come along. Little did I know those days were about to be over. I was instantly hooked, and my dating life changed dramatically.

Eventually Aunt Olivia joined a dating site. I was a struggling college student, so she allowed me to access her account with her user name and password. Since she didn't have any pictures on the website I just introduced myself to men I was interested in. I told them I was using my aunt's membership. I described myself and what I was looking for. If they were interested I asked them to email me at my personal email account. In 1996 I didn't see any pictures on this website so this process was no different than putting an ad in the classified. I was still very green to the whole World Wide Web process, so I enlisted a friend to give me the rundown since her brother was studying to be a computer engineer. After about a thirty minute tutorial in the school's computer lab, I was off and running. I came across an ad that caught my eye. I based my interest off his profile's bio; 25 years old, 6'2" tall, 220 pounds, and worked in publications. He had detailed descriptions of his likes, dislikes, and what he was looking for in a woman. His depiction of the woman for him sounded like music to my ears. I sent him an email. In less than a week we were talking on the phone, creating high phone bills. Remember long distance telephone rates in 1996 were entirely different than today's fees. There was no such thing as free nights and weekends or unlimited long distance home phone service providers.

I thought I had met the man of my dreams. We talked every day. After several weeks of build-up we decided to finally meet. He made the two and half hour trek to my campus and I was standing exactly where I told him I would. He drove up in a little Saturn. I was finally going to meet the man of my dreams in person. He was the man that played a starring role in all my fantasies. Unfortunately, my dream man turned into my date from hell. He parked the car and literally had to push himself off the steering wheel to extract himself from the vehicle. He was definitely 6'2 but had to be well over 400 pounds. I was flabbergasted and totally crushed. I wanted to run but my feet wouldn't move. I couldn't believe this was the same man I had talked to every day for two months. How could my mind play such tricks on me? Ok let's be clear, his weight was not the issue. Ok let me be honest it was an issue, but not the primary issue. The primary issue was his lie. I couldn't believe this man sat on the phone with me day after day knowing he lied to me from the beginning. He didn't even bother to warn me when we finally decided to meet. Its one thing to lie about 20 or 30 pounds, but 200 pounds was an entirely different story. I had fantasized about my dream man and was totally disappointed when my dream turned into a nightmare. He was a nice person and still had the personality that charmed me on the phone, but his personality wasn't enough for me to get past the deceit. I also wasn't attracted to him. Despite my reservations, I continued on the date saying to myself at least we could still be friends. His plans were totally different. As we were saying our good-byes in the lobby of my dorm, he leaned over to kiss me. Instinctively, I backed up. He was visibly upset and I noticed a change in his demeanor. Then he asked me directly what I thought of him. I was stunned. I searched my mind for an answer finally blurting out "You're bigger than I expected." I believed that was a reasonable answer. He did lie about having an extra two hundred pounds. Naturally, he began to argue and yell at me that I was shallow. I in turn yelled back, "You should never have lied; clearly you were hiding it for a reason." This taught me a lesson not to lie. I would never want to be in the same position he put himself in, on a date with someone who had no interest in me. Obviously that date didn't turn into a wonderful dating experience; however, it did turn into a wonderful Internet dating learning experience.

I didn't allow that one bad incident to deter me from my relationship goals. I continued Internet dating. Looking back on my Internet dating history, I've had some good dates, some bad dates, and some so-so dates. You aren't guaranteed anything when you meet new people. When my friends are sitting at home complaining about being alone, or involved in dead-end relationships because their low self esteem convinced them they will never find another man; I'm out on an adventure with a potential new boyfriend. I cherish my new experiences. Each new experience may lead to infinite possibilities. The world of online dating made me understand my self-worth. I realized I don't have to settle and neither do you.

When I look back on my first Internet experience, I had to ask myself a question.

Was He Really What I Was Looking For, Or Was He Just The Fantasy Of What I Wanted Him To Be?

Once I answered that question the reality of the situation was evident. I used my imagination to make him into what I wanted him to be. I had expectations before I actually met him.

I also had come to the realization that even though I tell the truth, the world is full of dishonest people. Everyone online does not believe in my same principles and values, and everyone's not looking for the same thing. The Internet makes it easy to fantasize about someone. I suggest you check your fantasies at the door. When meeting new people take them as individuals and as they come. Do not start putting his last name next to yours when you know nothing about him. Elevated expectations of someone you don't know can be very disappointing.

MEN

I know this goes without saying, but men are very different than women. We should all be aware of that nugget of information. Women are primarily lead by their needs and emotions. Men are logical creatures which sometimes makes it hard to connect. Men can also be more visual then women. I know quite a few men who want a beauty queen on their arm regardless of the woman's personality (remember the eighty nine year old man who married Anna Nichole Smith a twenty six year old stripper). Although women wouldn't mind having an attractive man by their side, we tend to use personality as a big factor in our dating choices. Fortunately for us not all men follow the beauty queen pattern. There are some men that are genuinely interested in your personality rather than your physical presentation.

Even Though Men Are Very Visual Don't Assume You Know What Every Man Wants Physically.

The male species physical desires can vary. Some men are into Big, Small, Short, Tall, White, Asian, Latino, or Black women. The common theme is that they see and like whatever they desire. Don't disregard yourself for fear of a lack of attraction from a man. I have met many men whose desires differ greatly from the standard beauty you see in a magazine or on a movie screen.

So you put yourself out there and receive an email from someone who's interested now what? Can you keep him after the initial attraction piqued his interest? Never make the mistake of questioning his interest in you.

The Worst Dating Mistake You Can Make Is To Talk Someone Out Of Going Out With You.

Several men have confided in me that they have met women that were beautiful on the outside, but once they started conversing with them, they found those women had trust issues, low self esteem or nasty personalities. Men fall all over her, but you can't understand why she can't keep a man. Being beautiful doesn't mean you don't have issues. Some women have traffic stopping looks; however, they have the worst self-esteem you've ever witnessed. Men who are truly looking for a connection care about your personality and who you are as a person.

Don't Be Fooled That All Beautiful Women Have Dating Mastered.

I lost a considerable amount of weight in my twenties. I went from a size 22 to a size 10. I have dated online at both body types. I found men that were interested in me when I was big and also small. Looking at me now you can't tell I used to have a major weight problem. Growing up with a weight problem diminished my self-esteem for a variety of reasons. How I felt about myself hindered me in the dating arena. I often questioned a man's interest so he would prove his feelings for me. This can be one of the most common side effects of low self esteem. Looking back on my life, not loving me put a monkey wrench in finding a man who would love me.

With every new person you meet, you are a clean slate. Don't assume you know what they are about and what they like. When you meet a man never make any negative comments about yourself. Self-deprecating humor isn't even funny when comedians do it, so don't try this at home folks. If the guy is interested in dating you leave it at that. Don't come up with a laundry list of your negative attributes expecting him to come to your defense. There's no such thing as a perfect person, and he should understand that too. I guarantee he's not perfect no matter what you think of him. You want a man who will love you unconditionally with all of your flaws, quirks and idiosyncrasies. Unfortunately, we women like to share entirely too much information about ourselves. Leave the sharing for girl's night out. When you initially meet a person, don't go into a long monologue about all your problems such as your weight problems, ill-mannered children, crazy exes, or financial troubles. Remember the key is not to talk a man out of dating you. Once you're in a committed relationship and he has developed feelings for you please by all means share until your heart's content. A complete stranger won't appreciate all that sharing, and will leave skid marks trying to get away from you.

The First Phase Of Internet Dating Is The Initial Attraction.

Through the exchanging of pictures you both can assess whether there is a mutual attraction before you initiate actual contact. If you write an award winning ad but choose not to upload a picture, then your ad could easily go unnoticed. Human nature requires us to want a visual (picture) first. There are many people who don't read the ad, and reply to you based on pure attraction so be prepared to answer questions that were clearly stated in your ad. Please don't take this as an insult. Minimally he's physically interested in you and that's the main reason for putting yourself out there. He could still turn out to be the man for you.

If you're that person who doesn't like taking pictures, and believe you're not very photogenic, GET OVER IT! Don't raid your old photo album to find a picture that clearly misrepresents what you currently look like. A picture weighing fifty pounds less or several years younger is not a good representation of what you look like now.

You Want To Represent Yourself In The Best Way Possible.

It's also a good idea not to post pictures with anyone else in them. You might look great in a group picture with your friends, but you don't want someone viewing your pictures and they're more interested in your friends than you. Another big mistake I hear men complain about is women who put up pictures with other men in them. They want to meet you so they shouldn't have to figure out who the guy in the picture is, even if he is your brother. I took a really awesome photo with a male friend of mine and posted the picture on a dating site. The guy had his arm around me so before I posted it I cut him out using photo shop. Since I received numerous questions regarding whose arm was around me I finally took the picture down. With all the inquiries I received concerning the picture, I can assume some men neglected to even send me a message because of that arm.

Call your friend find a digital camera, get yourself together like you're doing a photo shoot, and get ready for your close up. Go and get your hair done, buy a new outfit, and get your make-up done too. It's your day, so act like you're a model. Do whatever it takes to boost your self-confidence so that you can make your best impression. The beauty of digital cameras is you can delete what you don't like. You don't have to waste time developing film. Digital cameras are another great advancement in modern technology. What you need to process and understand is that how someone looks to the opposite sex is purely subjective. Meaning, it's on a case by case basis. I can't stress it enough beauty is in the eye of the beholder. Haven't you been out and about and noticed an unattractive person coupled with a very attractive person? Don't you always wonder to yourself, how the @3%$! did they get together? There's no true definition of beauty because everyone's opinion is different. Who's to say that attractive person doesn't look at that seemingly unattractive person and believe they are a god or goddess.

If you're totally against putting your pictures online, please understand that it's a commonly known fact that profiles with pictures get a lot more responses than those without. I totally understand the need for anonymity for some, but you should keep in mind you may be sabotaging your chances of meeting the man of your dreams just so your co-workers won't know your dating online.

Basic Dating Rules

1) Don't Come Across As Being Needy

  a. *Don't make multiple phone calls. Call then leave a message and allow him time to get back to you. If he's interested enough he will call you back.*

  b. *Don't request constant attention. Let him request your company. When he wants to spend time with you that's always a good sign. If he doesn't he won't ask to see you.*

  c. *Don't question his every move or tell him your every move. That's relationship behavior. Until you're in one don't make this a habit. You're casually dating and you need to keep it that way until you are in a relationship.*

d. *Don't always answer the phone. Let him
   believe you're busy and have a life of your
   own. It's very important not to allow
   him to believe he's your entire universe.
   Continue going out, enjoying life and
   talking to your friends. I had a friend who
   always had men with high level of interest
   in her. She told me men love busy woman.
   A woman who has a life is very attractive.
   Do not wait by the by the phone for him to
   pay attention to you. It is the thrill of the
   chase. If you are busy and grant him time
   in your life, he will feel privilege that you
   could spare the time to spend with him.*

2) Let him ask you out for the first date.

a. *When meeting someone online let the man
   make the first move to meet you. This will
   show his interest. If you really like this
   person and are ready to meet him do not
   try to manipulate him to ask you out. You
   want this man to want you, and not force
   anything. Let him be the man and show
   you his interest.*

3) Demand Respect

    b. *Never allow a man to treat you in a disrespectful manner. Get out of that situation immediately. It only leads to future disrespect.*

    c. *Never allow any man to step on your comfort zone. A lot of men treat the Internet like their own personal **1-900** number. If you come in contact with this behavior discontinue communication. Most websites have blocking capabilities. Use it when necessary.*

4) How Do You Know If He's Interested

    a. *When he stays in communication with you. Someone that you hear from every now and then is not showing enough interest.*

    b. *When he requests your time on a regular basis.*

    c. *When he makes you a regular part of his life, and introduces you to friends and family members.*

5) Make Him Pay For The First Date

    a. *Chivalry is not dead. If a man is interested in you he will have no problem paying for the first date.*

    b. *If he has financial problems do not turn down a walk in the park or meeting for coffee. He is still making an effort.*

    c. *Do not pass up the cheap date. When men are Internet dating more than likely they have gone on several dates. I have talked to men who use the Internet to date. They feel it can be expensive to take out all potential women. Some have adopted to start with a cheap date to see if they're interested before opening up their wallets.*

    d. *Do not accept a date who suggests meeting in an obscure location such as a gas station or Wal-Mart. If you agree to such a meeting you've placed yourself in the "I have low standards" category.*

6) Do Not Make The First Date At Either Parties Homes

    a. *This is very important. He is a stranger on the other end of a computer. You should be* cautious to let anyone in your home or go to someone's home you do not know. You may feel really comfortable with him through many conversations, but meet him and take the time to feel comfortable in person. Body language shows you a lot about a person. In person they can't mask themselves like on the other end of a computer or phone.

7) Do Not Have Sex With Him To Quickly

a. *This is an age old rule. Having sex can change the relationship or potential relationship greatly. I've had countless conversations with women after they are heartbroken. They really liked the guy they were seeing and had sex quickly. All of a sudden he's not answering the phone or his interest level diminished significantly. You keep the power by not giving your body to a man. Some women can be very emotional. If you're the emotional type of woman, sleeping with a man you like, but unsure of how he feels could turn out badly.*

b. *Men like the thrill of the chase. When he doesn't have to work for it, he could put you in the category of being easy and lose interest. Meaning he had no problem sleeping with you when you offered, but has no intentions of taking you home to meet his mom.*

c. *Some men can have you on the top of their list until sex comes too easily. I know in this day and age it's easy to think we're past those double standards. You would be surprised how many men still consider women whores if they have sex without making them do any work. Make him work for your affections.*

d. *All rules are meant to be broken. Every dating situation and relationship can be different. Not every situation is ruined by early intimacy. You need to gauge the situation. If sex is something you want to happen, you must be willing to take the risk to see how it turns out. Keep in mind it is a genuine risk where men are concerned.*

8) Do Not Introduce Him To Your Friends And Family Before A Relationship Is Established

a. *Men will run from women who desire an instant commitment. Putting this man in front of your family members can be interpreted as just that.*

b. *Parents can be unpredictable creatures. You don't want questions asked to this man about your relationship when a relationship hasn't been established.*

c. *Meeting your friends could be ok in certain settings. If you are giving a holiday party and invite him to join the festivities it's harmless. If you are having a couple's night that would not be the best move if you're not a couple.*

d. *I would not present all new potential men to your friends and family. If it doesn't work out you leave yourself open to advice, which you may not want to hear. The constant questions why it didn't work out can be very annoying after a while as well. Make him understand that you believe you're worth more of an effort. Don't ever lower your standards just to get a date. If he chooses not to comply with your rules, then he's not worth your time.*

9) Do Not Lie

a. *It can be easy on the Internet to fabricate things about yourself. There was a reality show that was on several years ago that followed people on their Internet dates. A woman went on a date with a man she was clearly interested in. After several dates she revealed that she lied about her profession and her name. The man was clearly upset and lost interest in her. No one wants to be*

*lied to. If there is some information you're
not ready to share then just say that. I do
not tell people where I work or live. I will
give them a general area of where I live
and my profession, but not the name of
the company I work for. If probed to give
more information I let them know I am not
comfortable enough to share such things.*

10)   Marriage On Your Mind

    *a. If you desire to be married wait to see
where his mind is before going into dream
wedding details. There are definitely men
online looking for marriage; however, you
want to avoid scaring off a man by giving
him the impression you would marry
anyone who asks.*

These are standard dating rules and in no way applies
to every situation; however these basic rules do stand true
in a great number of dating scenarios. I met a woman
who met a man online and was married in less than six
months, so the same could happen to you too.

Go With What Feels Right For You.

What Exactly Are You Looking For?

This is one of the most important questions you will ask yourself during this process. If you don't know your likes or dislikes or what you will and won't tolerate the online dating world can be very aggravating and frustrating. We would all like to jump on a computer and within the first ten minutes BOOM, we found our soul-mates. Granted that does happen from time to time, but most of the time it doesn't. I have a Vietnamese friend who joined a Vietnamese dating site. She met someone in the first ten minutes of being online. He lived in another state. They maintained a long distance relationship for two years and eventually got married. This certainly isn't the case for most people; however, it does happen. Have you decided what you're looking for in a mate? Leave all those criteria in general terms and leave room for adjustment. This list is something to work off of, not written in stone.

If Looks Are Important Then Always Require A Picture

If you've made pictures of yourself available it is only fair to require the same. You must make your request prior to engaging in long conversations with a possible love interest. If they don't have a picture you need to make a choice whether you wish to continue the conversation or not. You also have to take a few things under consideration. Some men are not into taking pictures. I've seen men put all kind of things online because they had no decent pictures of themselves. I've seen everything from driver's license pictures to high school yearbook photos (and the dude was 37). The first question to ask when you see their pictures is how recent is this photo? Before you throw that question out there make sure your pictures are always up to date.

Women can also be very deceiving when it comes to trying to meet a man. We have been known to post old pictures or pictures of relatives under the belief that once he gets to know us the deception of the photo will not be an issue. I strongly suggest you do not do that. Why would you want to pursue a man who really doesn't want you? They merely want the image of you that you put out there. Imagine how hurtful it will be when you meet someone after you've posted outdated photos and they're no longer interested. Personally it would be a huge blow to my self esteem to go out on a date and the guy looked at me like I had a third eye, and he didn't know where the hell I came from? I've heard so many horror stories from men whom go on dates and the person they were conversing with looked nothing like the pictures they viewed. Those men responded in various forms. Some of them left the women standing right where they met, others confronted them on the spot about the deceit, and the nicer men went through with the date only to never call her again. Like I stated earlier,

"Beauty Is In The Eye Of The Beholder"

You have to love yourself before anyone else can. As long as you exude confidence men will always be attracted to you and you will always catch your prey. Growing up I had a friend who wasn't very attractive with a severe weight problem (I know it's a terrible thing to say, but it's true nonetheless). I was always envious of her because she always had handsome boyfriends. Men paid a lot of attention to her and they lavished her with gifts. The difference between she and I was, she had confidence and I didn't. Every where she went, she commanded attention with her presentation of confidence. You couldn't tell this girl she didn't own a runway. That's how you're supposed to present yourself. You aren't displaying arrogance or snobbery, you're just confident. Confident doesn't mean putting down others to elevate yourself, or even stating how great you are. Bragging about your attributes shows you're trying to convince others of something you do not believe yourself. Confidence relies more on actions than words. It represents standing up for what you believe in, not allowing others to mistreat you, and showing the world that you're comfortable with and love yourself. Not every man was attracted to my friend. The few that didn't share her interest she acknowledged that it was their loss and moved on effortlessly.

The Worst Mistake We Make As Women Is We Don't Value Ourselves Unless Someone Puts Value On Us.

We allow our parents, friends and most likely a man to determine our value and worth. None of those people should have any say in how valuable you are. Unfortunately, this is the biggest error in judgment on our parts.

Loving Yourself Is The Most Important Thing You Can Do For Yourself.

You should always be first on your list of priorities. If you're not at that point in your life yet, then you need to start doing things for yourself to uplift your spirits. Go get your nails done. Go take a walk in the park. Recite positive affirmations to yourself daily. Do whatever it takes to make sure you show appreciation to yourself. If you don't start doing it for yourself, the first man that comes around to lift you up may turn out to be a wolf in sheep's clothing. Some men will prey on women with low self-esteem. I have seen several women fall into that trap. That type of man gets joy out of putting you down and taking from you. I am no stranger to working on self esteem. It took a lot of work on my part to love myself, but I have to say the benefits are worth it.

Ok, I've digressed. Let's get back to the posting of pictures debate. At times men will post profiles that describe themselves as very handsome, but they don't have any pictures. The question remains, handsome to whom? The person in question very likely may not be for you. When viewing pictures keep in mind people normally post the best pictures they have of themselves. He could have taken that picture on a good day at a great angle. I'm guilty of the same offense. If I don't look my best in a picture, it ends up getting deleted from my digital camera. So if he looks 20-25% worse than his picture would you still go out with him? If the answer is yes then continue with your dialogue. When meeting a person face to face you may feel they look better or worse than their picture. To avoid this negative occurrence use the 20-25% rule when assessing attraction. I met a man online and his picture looked like he came out of GQ magazine. When I met him in person it was clear the GQ picture was taken a good thirty pounds ago, but I still found him attractive and we dated for two years.

Word of caution please don't fall for the line, I'm not ugly when chatting with someone that doesn't want to send you a photo. If he doesn't have one posted then your next question should be "please email me one." If he still uses the line "I don't have any pictures but I'm not ugly", then he's probably ugly or at the least very insecure about his looks. Furthermore, there's an even greater possibility that you might not even be attracted to him at all. There are many success stories where women have met men online they weren't initially attracted to. That can be a major risk in the time management department if looks are important to you. It has happened to me. Once upon a time I met this man who was at least three inches shorter than I and very skinny. As a general rule, I tend to never date men that are smaller than I am. I have phobia of looking like his mother. This skinny short man was attractive but clearly not my type at all. He showed up to our date with flowers which I thought was a very sweet gesture. I continued the date despite my reservations about his size. The date actually turned out to be a lot of fun and we wound up dating for several months afterwards. I fell for his personality not his appearances. It's a very strong possibility that your dream man won't come neatly packaged in the wrapping that you picked out, rather in another form altogether. If you want dating success you must always keep an open mind.

He Might Not Be What You Pictured, But He May Turn Out To Be The Best Thing That Ever Happened To You.

If you're confident about your desires and you don't want to entertain men you're not attracted to, never go forward without a picture. Again, be prepared to trade yours as well.

When posting photos, don't post a picture that presents you in a manner you don't want to be presented in. You always want to present yourself with class. We're all aware that sex sells so that leads us to believe sexy pictures will attract a man. Sexy pictures will attract men. If you want to be painted in a sexual light then by all means post sexy pictures, but if that's not your desire then I strongly advise against it. If you're only interested in casual sexual encounters then sexy photos may be appropriate. Do not post any provocative pictures with your breasts prominently displayed, or wearing a bikini. Men tend to respect those that respect themselves.

If You Don't Want Men To Approach You In A Sexual Manner COVER IT UP!

I've had many conversations with men who claimed some women looked easy or like a prostitute in their pictures. They in turn asked those women when they could hook up (casual sexual encounter). Naturally the women were offended by their blatant sexual advances. Those men felt justified by their approach because of the pictures that were posted.

You are going to be approached by men that don't interest you. You are going to receive offensive emails. At times you are going to have to delete and block a profile altogether. These options come standard on all dating web-sites and its common practice. Don't feel bad if you have to block a user because you're comfort level is more important than their feelings. There's no truer statement for online dating than the old saying "you may have to kiss a few frogs to find your prince."

Whatever Necessary Information You Need To Know About A Potential Man Before Dating Him, Make Sure You Ask Up Front.

If marital status, number of children, or smoking and drug use are important issues, don't wait until you really like a guy to obtain this information.

I believe the only question you shouldn't ask someone out right is how much money they make. Everything else is fair game. Why waste your time getting to know someone only to find out they aren't legally divorced or they are a recreational drug user. If you can't move forward unless you know his income status, then ask him what he does for a living and research the general salary of that profession in the state where he lives. Keep in mind how much money a man makes is based upon several factors and is relative to their financial situation. Here's an illustration to explain what I'm talking about:

You meet a man who makes $70,000 a year but has three kids from a divorce. More than likely his child support payments and possible alimony takes a generous portion of his $70,000 income.

You meet another man that also makes $70,000 but he's in a lot of debt. That $70,000 can feel like $20,000 with all the bills he has to pay.

If your qualifications for your dream man are contingent upon his salary, you may very well meet a man that looks the part, but his numerous creditors has him living one paycheck away from homelessness. Getting that deep into a man's business just to go on a date is a little extreme, so I would just accept the first date and see how it goes.

If you meet a guy and you're unsure about his background but like him, there are many websites that allow you to access personal information. I wouldn't waste your time or money conducting background checks on every date you have. After you've spent a significant amount of time getting to know someone you are dating, I would invest in the websites if red flags come up. It could be worth the money to check him out. Don't just dismiss your feelings as paranoia due to some previous bad experiences because you may very well be on to something. There are websites that will give you property, marriage, and criminal history information. A friend of mine had a cousin who was dating a guy she met online. She was in love with this man but her family believed something wasn't right about him. The family invested money in an online background search. Subsequently, they found out he was married and had spent a considerable amount of time in prison. Believe me they felt the money they spent was worth every dollar. There are also a few free basic investigation sites available. If he gives you a home telephone number you can do a reverse phone number search and find the address connected to that particular phone number. My rule of thumb is, if you don't feel like spending the money; leave him alone if you're not getting a good vibe from the situation and it just doesn't feel right.

When in doubt follow your instincts and use your gut. You really have to be attentive of people you meet online; however, you should also use that attentiveness when meeting new people in general. I dated a man for several months and felt he was lying about the home he claimed to own. I confided in a friend about my misgivings and she informed me that property records were public information. She directed me to a website for the county of the residence. I typed in his address and to my dismay I was correct he did not own the house. I didn't care whether he owned property or not. Lying is just something I cannot tolerate. My belief is that if someone is capable of lying about the little things, then they are capable of lying about anything. Trust is the most important thing on my list of what I want in a man. Men lie for a variety of reasons. Some men lie to make a good impression. Then there are also the married men whom lie because they want to cheat on their wives. Some married men are upfront about their relationship and intentions whereas others hide their marital status. I have no interest in being the other woman in any capacity. When approached by these men I politely decline their invitation to converse, or when the truth is revealed I let them know I'm not interested. Several years ago, I dated a man for a few months and noticed I never received an invitation to his house. That was very suspicious to me. My house was always the meeting ground. I was determined to get to his house to investigate so I could find out if he was married or at the very least living with a woman. My suspicions were squashed when I finally reached his house. I asked to use the rest room and did a little snooping that eased my tension; it was obvious that a woman did not live there. If you feel something is not right investigate. You do not want to be in a situation where trust is an issue.

If You Feel Things Are A Little Shady Take A Closer Look.

Preferences

Being cautious should not be exclusive to the Internet. It's amazing how many women have met men on the street, and immediately gave them directions to their house. You don't know any more about that individual on the street than if you met him online. I'm not suggesting you live your life in complete fear of everyone you meet, just be smart about it. There are a lot of liars, con artists and other predators out there. You don't want to invite any unnecessary drama into your life or become another statistic.

When it comes to finding a mate physical attributes you desire is one aspect of the selection process. You also have to determine your other personal preferences. You'll need to decide if you don't mind if he has children or pets? Do you mind if he plays video games all day? Do you mind if he's a sports fanatic? Do you mind if he's a workaholic? All of these attributes are your personal choice. I have a girlfriend in her mid thirties who for whatever reason refuses to date men with children. That's her right, but remember the more specific your requirements the less people you have to choose from.

When Creating Your List You Should Rank Order Your Areas Of Importance.

I have a dog, so I prefer my mate be an animal lover, but if he doesn't it's not a deal breaker for me.

Every woman's version of a perfect man is different and usually needs to be redefined with realistic terms. We all want to believe those fairytales told to us as children. Those books gave us the dream of a fictional perfect man coming to our rescue and sweeping us off our feet. When dating we need to stay in reality and not in fantasy.

A friend of mine married a man with three children from his previous marriage. She was hesitant to at first because she felt like he had too much baggage. Now they are happily married and she could have allowed a good man to slip away based upon his past relationship. Let's face it everyone has a past including you. If you can't deal with children then stick to what you ultimately want so you won't feel like you're settling for less than what you really want. I would describe your preferences in this manner:

I would prefer a man without children. The most I could accept is two if they are well behaved, but anymore than that is out of the question.

I stated what I like, what I'm willing to accept, and what I would not except. When you're creating your list of preferences express your requirements in that manner. You won't waste your time and you'll achieve your desired dating goals whatever they may be. Remember the Internet is your means of alleviating those lonely weekends. It will help prevent you from having to hang out with your girlfriends when you know you would rather be out on a date. If you try online dating you won't have to continue wishing you had a man interested in you.

Do you want a relationship that leads to marriage? If that's your desire then you must open up your world. The average person goes to work, home, gym and maybe church. Thus you run into the same people day after day. Your soul mate can be in your day to day life, but he also might not be. Online dating increases your odds by opening the door of possibilities (infinite possibilities). I once asked a Christian therapist what he advised his female patients who desired to be married. How does he guide them? He said, "I tell these women to date as many men as possible and weed them out according to how they meet there standards." He then told me that the majority of those women were married within a year or two. I took his advice to heart and incorporated it into my dating life.

I have a friend who's never had an active dating life. She's thirty six years old and has gotten comfortable with being alone. Yes you can get used to being alone. She wanted a man in her life but resigned herself to the possibility of being alone for the rest of her life. I do believe some people like to be alone. That's fine for people who desire that, but most people don't want to be by themselves, they've just accepted it. On numerous occasions I suggested she join a dating site. She was strongly against it, but eventually gave in after months of prodding. Now she's been with her boyfriend for six months, and the crazy thing is he lives in her sub division. Can you imagine meeting a man who lived just around the corner the entire time? She lived there for six years and never seen him before their date. I had a similar situation. I met a neighbor online and we've been close friends since. We never dated but a good friendship resulted from our meeting. Do not discount that possibility. Every man you meet online might not be in line to be your husband. Do not exclude the possibility of friendship. I have met several men online where a friendship was created. They have even introduced me to their friends who they felt I might be interested in. Even if you do not believe it, life has the capabilities of six degrees of separation. You never know Mr. Right may be two streets over but you may never have an opportunity to cross paths.

Most Women Make The Mistake Of Meeting One Man And Focusing All Of Their Attention On Him.

In some situations that method may work. A lot of times it doesn't. Take your time and enjoy dating. Don't put all your eggs in one basket. If you're the type, that doesn't like to date more than one person a time that is fine. Do what is comfortable to you. Do not focus all of your time on him. Continue having a life outside of your dating relationship. If it doesn't work out just start all over again. You also need to be aware if you're meeting men online you're not guaranteed to be the sole holder of his dating card. That's ok because you're only casually dating and should have no expectation unless you enter into a relationship. Once you have mastered this art form, you will cross over into the realm of finding the right one for you. That may happen in your first click of the mouse and it might not. The key is to enjoy the process and stay positive.

The Wrong Man

Why do a lot of women stay in relationships with the wrong man? Here are some of the primary reasons I believe women use as an excuse to stay with the wrong guy:

1) They're bored

I know several people who are in relationships just to pass the time. They have no real interest in the man but keeping him around is comfortable. They could be blocking their blessing for true happiness.

2) There's no one else available to date

I have also fallen into this trap to give myself an excuse for staying in a relationship. I had a belief that no one else was out there. I stayed in a relationship I know longer wanted to be in just to have someone in my life.

3) Mr. Right seems unobtainable, so they'd rather have a piece of a man than none at all

I know several women in relationships where they are subjected to verbal or physical abuse. They deal with lazy men who contribute nothing to them or their household. Abuse is nothing to live with in any way. If someone is knocking you down and do not contribute to the emotional elevation of your life it's time to move on.

4) They have low self-esteem

A lot of women suffer from self-esteem issues. I have struggled with it myself. This can be very destructive in dealing with men. Self-esteem issues can prevent you from choosing the man you deserve, and makes it easier to settle for something less. When you feel good about yourself it is easier not to deal with a loser. Not all attention is good attention.

5) You're waiting around for him to marry you

I know a woman who dated the same guy for seven years. After two proposals (with engagement rings) and no marriage on the horizon he's still stringing her along. In order for this not to occur in your life, you have to believe there's something better for you. I know another woman who dated a guy for several

*years and she wanted to get married and he
didn't. Eventually she left him, met someone
new, and was married within a year. Another
friend of mine wanted to get married to a
man she dated for two years. She was ready
for marriage and he wasn't. She decided she
was worth more. He would have to learn to
live without her. She broke off the relationship.
Six months later he was at her door step with
a ring. You have to be able to walk away from
a relationship. Don't give someone else power
over your life. You're worth so much more than
that.*

My grandmother always said,

"Anything That's For You Is For You."

You shouldn't have to convince or coerce a man into
marrying you. He should want to. If you desire to be
married, forcing a man to walk down the aisle isn't the
best method of achieving your goal. If the man you're
dating doesn't share your goals for the relationship you
have to accept that and walk away. A close friend of
mine dated a man for two years. She desperately wanted
to become his wife; however, the relationship ended on
a bad note. To add insult to injury he was engaged to
someone else within six months.

Unfortunately, we as women make a lot of concessions to remain in our relationships. Even though we want a romantic man, a man that has similar interests, a man that puts our needs before theirs, and someone that really cares about us, but we often settle for less. We all have our pre-conceived preferences, yet those desires go out the window for some of the following reasons:

1) **I love him and want to marry him. If he just changed certain things about himself he would be perfect.**

> *Ladies you can't change a man. You cannot go into a relationship believing that you have the power to change someone. If you've spent enough time with him, he's shown you exactly who he is. Please pay attention. If you can't accept him as is, then you should move on. If your man is a slob and you're a clean freak, then you can pretty much expect to be the maid in your relationship.*

2) **I'm not happy but I don't want to be alone.**

> *It is better to be alone than in a bad relationship. Don't be afraid to be by yourself. The right man for you could be out there, but you might be blocking your blessings by hanging on to a dead end relationship. Many women don't*

get rid of one man until they find another one to replace him. This isn't the best method of dating although it's a common practice by both genders. An inability to be alone is a major character flaw. Taking time off in between relationships allows you to learn more about yourself to make better relationship choices. It's never a good thing to use the next man that comes along as an excuse to leave your present relationship. You shouldn't need any excuses to leave a bad relationship. Just do it. I have a friend who can't be alone. So she constantly replaces one relationship with another and always has problems with the next relationship. She never takes the time to teach herself how to make better decisions when selecting men. She's always looking for the next man to love her because she doesn't love herself. When they don't live up to her standards she starts aggressively looking for his replacement. I've often told her that she's merely rotating the trash.

My take on Internet dating is if you see any red flags move on. It's so easy to move on because there are so many other men online. Once you realize this, moving on will become easier and easier.

You're Looking For Mr. Right Not Mr. Right Now.

Looking For Casual Sex

Casual sex is not a new phenomenon. I've had my share of casual sexual encounters. It is a false statement that women don't have sexual desires like men.

I met a man online that turned out to be a good friend. We never dated because it was clear he wasn't looking for a relationship just sexual encounters. I didn't share his same aspirations, but we continued to talk anyway. He was generally a decent guy, but he just wasn't looking for anything serious. He was newly divorced and didn't desire a relationship. He would share stories of his encounters with the women he would meet for his sexual escapades. They were all professional women some single, married, with children, or without children. Society leads us to believe that people looking for casual sex online are perverse; however, they can be your average everyday person. If you have these desires believe me there are people out there just like you.

I have a friend who constantly whines about needing sex. She wishes she had a man in her life just to have sex with. You can get physical pleasure without a soul mate. I suggested that until her soul mate shows up, she doesn't have to remain physically unsatisfied day after day. She can find a man to handle her sexual maintenance. There have been periods in my life where I remained abstinent and refrained from casual sexual encounters when I wasn't in a relationship. I didn't complain during that time period because it was a choice I made. Sex is the easiest thing to get if you want it, and not something worth complaining about. We're all adults, so handle your business.

A friend of mine has a young buck that she regularly has sex with on a casual basis. I joke with her and call her a Cougar because he is over ten year younger than her. She's not in a relationship. She has three children and runs her own business. She has no time for anything other than the occasional pass thru to handle her needs. There's no shame in it. We're all grownups, so you needn't be worried about being labeled a whore in the high school locker room.

No One Needs To Know
Your Business.

If you're the type of woman that can't separate sex from love, I strongly advise against this practice. If a sexual encounter creates instant feelings; casual sex is not for you. Additionally, if you are looking for a relationship and you settle for casual sexual encounters instead of having a relationship then you will suffer emotional discontent with your situation. Casual sex is momentary gratification that cannot replicate a relationship. Men are predators and think with instinct and logic, women tend to act on emotions and how something makes them feel. There are men and women that can totally switch these roles; however, that's normally not the case. Some women can have sex and enjoy the moment without any emotional attachments, yet others who have sex and are instantly attached. If you're the emotional after sex type, a vibrator might be a better choice. A toy will spare you a lot of emotional drama and heartache. Emotions can lead you to make bad decisions. If you're involved just for sex, usually that's all your partner is interested in as well, not a long term relationship. You need to be clear which one you want before dabbling with casual sex.

Here's the secret. Have casual sex with the man you don't want to be in a relationship with and not with the man you do. Most men will hate that bit of advice because of the double standard involved. You see ALL men have women they sleep with and women they marry and most of the time it's not the same woman. They would never suggest we do the same; however, I suggest we should.

You also have to take it under consideration some male egos will never accept it if you've had more sexual partners. One day a group of girlfriends and I were discussing how we answered the question, "How many men have you slept with?" One of my friends said "five". I said, "Umm, you slept with more than five before you left high school." She replied, "True, but if I told him the real number he would probably dump me." She made a very valid point. Having a high number of past sexual partners doesn't make you a bad person. It is what it is. Some men don't understand the mantra "Don't ask the questions you don't want the answer to." My normal response to that question when asked is,

"I'm Not Answering That Question."

I often get negative feedback from the guy that wants the answer and they usually accuse me of having a lot of baggage. My other response is, "It's neither relevant nor important and what does my past have to do with you? Do you want to be my past or my future?" If a man can't handle that response, then I usually lose interest. I ask the question, "If he's so consumed by my past will he ultimately judge me for it." I'm open-minded and I expect my mate to be as well, so judgment is not something I want to be a part of.

There Are Some Exceptions To The Casual Sex Rule.

Believe it or not some relationships can be born from a strictly sexual arrangement. If you have any sexual fetishes, the Internet can connect you with many people who share those same needs. Who knows, a relationship could emerge. A friend of mine married a man she slept with on the first date and they were involved in a "just sex" relationship for a year. Then they got married. The best advice I can give is do whatever makes you comfortable and be yourself. Don't apologize for who you are. There's always going to be a double standard. Men that sleep around are praised and called a stud, whereas women are ridiculed and called a tramp. Don't worry about what other people say or think. You're an adult and you have every right to do whatever feels right to you. No matter what you do in life until the day you die someone's going to talk about you. I got some great advice from my mother once. She said, "Do what makes you happy because when you go to the grave you will be going alone."

Predators

So you've decided that you want to casually date and perhaps engage in a fling or two, but you must beware of Internet predators. Unfortunately, there are a lot of predators online. We've all seen the news where people come up missing or murdered after meeting someone online. These occurrences are very real and extremely dangerous. To protect yourself you must use common sense at all times. You also have to use your gut instincts when you're getting to know someone. If you venture into finding a sexual partner online you need to be very observant of people to prevent yourself from being harmed. If something doesn't feel right don't risk it. Here's a suggested step to follow to avoid putting yourself in harms way:

Get As Much Personal Information As Possible On Him.

Before you go out on your date, share all of that information with another person. Whether it's his telephone number, place of business, or home address make sure a third party can find you if necessary. It's also a good idea to let someone else know exactly where your date is taking you, especially if you decide to ride with him (which I don't recommend until you are comfortable). When you meet him write down his license plate number or vehicle make and model and forward that information to a friend via text or phone. Until you get used to meeting men online you should never go out on a date without telling someone you trust and let them know which web-site you met the person on. I know you probably don't want people all in your dating business, but no one wants to be on unsolved mysteries either. Pick one person you trust and make sure they are informed about your whereabouts. After every new date I call a friend and let her know I got home safely. Make sure you let your date know you gave out his personal information to a third party. If he had plans of harming you, he may think twice about it if he knows he could be easily tracked down.

As a single woman you should always come prepared with condoms.

HIV/AIDS Is Very Real And Extremely Dangerous.

Part of being sexually involved with someone is running the risk of catching a sexually transmitted disease (STD) or getting pregnant, so you're responsible for protecting yourself. Not only are there murderous predators online, but there are also plenty of men with diseases they have no intention of disclosing to you. HIV and AIDS are potentially lethal diseases, but those are not the only ones to be worried about. There are other non-lethal STD's that can potentially change your life. Herpes and Genital Warts are two very common incurable STDs that can infect you even while using a condom. My advice is to turn on the lights and do a visual inspection of his genitals. If you see any rash or anything that looks suspicious I suggest you rethink having sex with that person. This isn't a guarantee you won't contract a disease, but it's better than nothing. You may also request the two of you go together and get STD testing done. I know it sounds a bit extreme for a casual sexual encounter, but the technology is out there and your results can be made available within a week. The bottom line is,

Don't Ever Have Sex Without A Condom!

Lady's please be careful. The Internet can provide you with unlimited sexual opportunities if that's what you're looking for, but it can also provide you with more than what you bargained for. There are just as many dangers as pleasures waiting for you. It's a well known fact that the advent of the Internet increased incidents of criminal sexual behavior such as rape and murders. If you love your life as much as I love mine. You'll watch your step and don't put yourself in any compromising positions.

Cheating

Believe it or not, there are websites that specifically cater to people who desire to cheat on their mate. When dating online there is always a possibility that the potential man is not single. Some men tell you this information up front and others don't disclose that information. Women also have used the Internet to cheat on their men, so it is not exclusive to the male species. If you want some kind of anonymity, the Internet can provide that. This has made the Internet used for cheating very prevalent. We already know my personal opinion on this subject. If you're not happy in a relationship you should leave for yours, and the other persons benefit. If leaving your relationship is not an option and you choose to cheat be careful.

Common Cheating Mistakes

These are examples of things to look out for if you suspect someone of cheating. This list can also be used to avoid getting caught cheating.

1) Personal Computers

If you are using the Internet to cheat, don't use the family computer. I have met people who have been caught cheating because their mate added a spyware to their home computer. This software can provide your partner every website you visited and even what you typed in an email message. I also suggest regularly deleting your cookies and temporary Internet files (TIF) on whatever computer you choose to use for cheating.

2) Cell Phones

If you have a family cell phone plan you probably don't want to contact the person you are cheating with on that phone. Your partner can always call the cell phone provider to find out who you are talking to.

3) Discretion

If you are cheating I would make it a practice to limit the amount of personal information the person you're cheating with has. Never let them know where you work or live. I have heard countless stories of the "other" person showing up at someone's place of business or home. You never know what a person is capable of doing. You don't want to be put in a compromising position with the man you are with and the man you are just sleeping with.

4) Cheating with someone who is also cheating

If you are cheating on someone who is also cheating make sure they are also being careful. I can't tell you the number of women who have contacted me over the years to inform me that I was with their man. Of course, I had no knowledge of that fact so I was always surprised when I received those phone calls. You do not ever want to find yourself in a compromising position with someone else's mate.

5) Routine change

People who suspect their partners are cheating usually get a gut feeling about it. The gut feeling sometimes comes with routine changes in your behavior. For example, suddenly you are always on the phone having private conversations. If you have never displayed that kind of behavior this could make your partner somewhat suspicious. Additionally, if you're usually a homebody but all of sudden you're extremely busy and constantly have things to do, you may also trigger suspicions from your mate.

In the past, I had an experience that totally blew my mind. I went out on one date with this guy I met online. The date wasn't particularly special and I decided to never call him again. While I was at the gym I received a strange call from a woman asking if I knew someone named Marcus. I had no idea what she was talking about and immediately called her back. She informed me that I went out on a date with her fiancé Marcus. She had hired a private investigator and knew exactly when and where we met. I didn't know who she was talking about at first because he told me his name was Mark. She was actually a really nice person and we spent almost an hour on the phone. I told her I had no interest in her man. Even though she had information on several women Marcus was cheating with, from the tone of the conversation, it was clear she was not ready to let him go. Then she informed me that she already spoken with another woman's husband Marcus had been dating and it sounded like she successfully broke up that marital relationship. I don't know the outcome of that situation, but it was too messy and dramatic for me.

Protecting Yourself

Emotionally

Remember the people you meet online are complete strangers. You owe each other nothing in terms of time and attention. My friend who was an Internet dating virgin got upset and was frustrated when a man she regularly spoke with suddenly stopped calling, and wouldn't return any of her calls. She went through all kinds of emotional tirades because the phone didn't ring. I tried to explain to her there are plenty of fish in the sea. My advice was to keep it moving because just as easily as you met him, you can meet someone else. Ladies, it takes too much time and energy to figure out why someone's not interested in you and it also doesn't really matter. He's not the right person for you, so acknowledge and move on. Don't get me wrong, I understand it's easy to become attached to someone you've been dating or even conversing with for an extended period of time. I suggest you don't get yourself caught up. State your desires and if that person doesn't live up to them let him go. If a man doesn't call you and won't return your calls, that's usually a clear indication he's not interested. Go back online and see what new emails you have waiting on you from other possible suitors.

I use the terminology Faders for those men that disappear out of your life without clear warning. It's so easy to fade in and out of people's lives on the Internet. Here today and gone tomorrow. Most women I talk to have a hard time dealing with Faders. Generally they are the type of women with limited dating experience, or the type that spend an extensive period of time trying to convince a man she's the right woman for him. When you call someone and they don't return your call let it go. I make two calls within a two week period, leave two messages and wait a week. If I don't hear from him after my efforts, I delete them from my cell phone. Men aren't complicated creatures. If they like you they'll show you, and they will make an effort. Here's an example: I dated this guy whom I adored, but he apparently didn't have the same feelings for me. I wanted him and that's what kept us together. I did all these special things for him which he enjoyed, but never showed any appreciation. Eventually he broke up with me and treated the new girl like a queen. Of course, my question was,

"So What Was Wrong With Me?"

There was nothing wrong with me. When I initially noticed he wasn't putting the same effort into me that I was putting into him, I should have gotten rid of him. Instead I doted on him and felt empty because he didn't reciprocate. When you keep a man around who doesn't display your same amount of interest you're self-esteem will get tarnished. I am not an emotionless creature. When someone I am interested in does not share my feelings it can hurt. I just do not let that emotion control me or tarnish my self-esteem in any way. I approach it as another dating learning experience and recognize that he was not the right person for me.

Lose His Number Immediately.

All men should be dealt with in this manner. Sometimes when you stop giving him all your attention he might come back around new and improved, but you shouldn't wait for that to happen. You should just move on. When dating you need to have clear standards of what you want and what you expect. Even though it's hard to appreciate witnessing someone fade out your life, someone you have a connection with that disappeared may have taught you a lot about dating and men. Most men won't give you the courtesy of informing you they aren't interested. They will simply ignore you and expect you to take the hint. Believe me, there is a man out there for you and the Fader just wasn't the one. If he doesn't want to be bothered with you, than it's his loss.

Reasons To Lose His Number!

1) He never calls me and I always call him.

A man that is interested in you will keep in touch. It won't take you long to figure out if he's interested it will be obvious. If you believe you do all the calling and he doesn't always answer the phone or acts disinterested when you call, stop calling him. Let him make the effort to call you. If the phone doesn't ring you got your answer.

2) He never asks me to go out.

There could be several reasons for this behavior. He could be arrogant and believes he doesn't have to put forth any effort. He could also be a homebody who prefers being at home. This could be a problem if you like going out. You may also need to speak up and tell him you would like to go out. He can't read your mind. If he doesn't offer to go out after you've mentioned it once or twice, let it go because he doesn't plan on taking you anywhere.

3) After we had sex his behavior changed.

Beware of this sign! He may have only wanted sex in the first place. If that is the case that is why his interest level disappeared once he got what he wanted. He also may have gotten comfortable and he doesn't believe he has to try as hard; you already gave him the booty prize. Act like it doesn't bother you in the least. This can be emotionally painful, you need to lift your head up and put him in the loser category. If he doesn't make the same efforts as before leave him alone.

4) His friends are more important than I am.

This is a very tricky subject. Some men are very attached to their friends. If he's more interested in his friends than you, I would probably leave him alone. If they're true friends they won't cease being his friend just because he has a new woman in his life. Now ladies let's be real if he always watches football with his friends on a certain night, don't take this as a sign he's not interested. You shouldn't try to pry a man from his friends. You'll seem very needy if you require his attention every waking hour. Let him have his friends and you have yours. If he consistently chooses his friends over you then there is a problem.

5) His mom has too much control over his life.

A woman once said to me "To understand how a man will treat you, observe how he treats his mom." In some respects that's a very true statement. If this man is still hanging on his moms left tit and she controls every aspect of his life there is a problem. **BEWARE** *if she has too much input regarding his personal affairs.* **BEWARE** *if they share the same living quarters.* **BEWARE.** *You could be involved with a Mama's Boy. Every woman wants to date a man that treats his mother with kindness and respect, but no one wants a Mama's Boy. You could potentially have a lifetime of not just dealing with him but also his mother. Becoming seriously involved with this type of man could have problems, especially if you don't get along with his mother. Think before you leap on that one.*

6) He never makes time for me.

Don't ever allow a man to use the tired excuse "I've been busy" because people make time for what they want. We all have careers and social lives and families. No one is that damn busy that they can't return a phone call. If he feeds you that line, I normally say, "Well then you probably shouldn't be trying to date me if you don't have time for me. Call me when your schedule frees up." Either he'll stop calling altogether, or he'll schedule some quality time quickly. If he's not that interested, he'll get offended by your bravado and stop calling. I have had countless conversation with men trying to make me understand why I am not a priority. Their arguments include, I don't want a man with goals. I don't understand all the things they have to do. I feel I am a very understanding person. I just don't want to date someone and still feel single because I never connect with them. On the other hand, don't ever make a man feel bad for spending time with his children or handling his responsibilities when he's not making time for you. This can be a fine line. Maybe you shouldn't date a man with children if you can't share their father with them. The key is quality time not quantity.

7) **Adopt the rule of two.**

Give a man two phone calls and two weeks. If he does not get back to you lose his number. If he is interested in you he will at least maintain communication with you. I don't care how busy he is. Men make time for what they want. If he is interested and uses the excuse of being busy to place you on the backburner, then you will always be on the backburner to everything else while with him. If you desire to be a priority in someone's life then do not accept this behavior. If he is interested in you he will make the adjustment to fit you in his life. If you are still interested in him even though he is not putting you on his list of priorities treat him in the same way. Do not make someone a priority that does not do the same for you.

You can always create your own list of what's important to you. These are just basic guidelines. The bottom line is,

You Don't Have To Stand For Crap.

It also shows you're aware of your power and self worth and that you're willing to walk away. If walking away isn't something you're good at, you need to work on that. Unfortunately it's an integral part of dating. When a relationship hasn't developed with your person of interest take the hint and move on. Continue casually dating other men until you find the one for you. When someone else is taking up your time it's easy to let go mentally of the man who didn't want to be bothered with you. Some men have a tendency to keep you around even if they are not that interested. Before changing your lifestyle to suit any man, you need to make sure you are on the same page. When you're ready to get into a serious relationship with someone, you need a definitive answer to the question, "do you see us having a future together"? You never want to wake up two years down the road and discover you're the woman he's with until the right one shows up.

Internet dating aids in the "Mrs. Right Now" dilemma because it increases the amount of people you come in contact with. When you use the Internet as a dating tool it may also increase the number of men that fade out of your life. If you're not the type of person who can handle that, you might have a few problems with online dating. If you're the type of woman who can't let a man you're interested in go or have actually stalked a man who wasn't interested. You too will have problems with Internet dating.

For those of you who can't see yourself participating in this type of behavior, here are some examples: You called the man so much he turned his cell phone off. You did a drive by of his house to see if he was there. You showed up somewhere uninvited. You called women in his phone to see what their relationship entailed. These are all bad business for dating. If you have to conduct yourself in that manner, I can assure you he's not the right man for you. You shouldn't have to go through all those changes for a man. Naturally I've made pit stops at all of those psycho places. Needless to say, those weren't the finest moments in my life. I don't believe that I'm crazy; I was just in emotional pain at those moments. In my mind that particular guy was the man of my dreams. I really should have taken a step back and realized that the man of my dreams should desire me. That's the moral to the story. You want him to want you and show it as well.

STOP CHASING MEN!

Anything you chase will run away. When you want someone you can't have it can intensify the need to have him.

Have you ever pushed away a man who was interested in you? He showed clear interest by always calling, and always requested to spend time with you. Your interest level was nonexistent because you weren't physically attracted to him. You didn't pay him much attention, but let him continue to try. He was fueled by the thrill of the chase and you let him believe it was possible that he had a chance to catch you.

Then here comes the man you're actually interested and you chase him. The key question is how to get the man you desire to have the same level of interest in you? Men love the thrill of the chase. Once they catch you, they will feel you're a worthy prize because they had to work hard to get you. This process only works if a man is interested in you. If the interest exist this just helps to increase his level of interest and have him pursue you instead of you pursuing him. You also need to identify that when the interest is not there, you need to let him go. This is the hardest part of dating.

I met a man I thought was my soul mate. We were friends and my feelings developed into something more and I thought we were on the same page. At least, that's what I thought. Once I realized he did not share my same level of interest it was hurtful to let him go. He would have happily remained friends and kept me around as long as I allowed it, but I wanted to be more than a friend. I made the choice to leave the situation because I knew remaining in his life would be a waste of my time. I knew that remaining hopeful that he would eventually feel the same way, would only lead to missed opportunities with someone else.

Don't Waste Your Time With Someone Who Lacks Interest In You.

Dating men online can be closely related to speed dating. A lot of potential datable men can pass through your life. The initial contact begins with an email or phone call. It also makes it possible for you to stop receiving new communication if you don't want any. It's easy to disappear when you don't want to be bothered. You can also use this to your advantage when you meet someone that is your type. You can simply ignore their emails or tell them you're not interested without the drama of explaining and justifying your decision. The beauty of online dating is: you don't have to explain yourself.

> **Men Are Like Buses One Is Certain To Come Around In Another Fifteen Minutes.**

If you find one undesirable or he doesn't live up to your standards just wait for the next bus.

Personal Information

It is impossible to successfully date online without giving out some personal information about yourself. You must be cautious of what information you give until you feel comfortable with the person. Protection of personal information should be a priority for several reasons:

1) Identity theft is on the rise

You can watch the news and see people going through the trash or hacking into computer systems to get your credit card or banking information. On the worldwide web there are people performing the same fraudulent activities. **Never give out your user names or passwords to anything.**

2) Internet predators try to gain information about you to harm you

In this day and age it is apparent that not everyone is out for your best interest. There are men who use the Internet to do harm to you. That's why you should always practice safe dating practicing until you know who you are dealing with. Do not give out your address or work location until you feel comfortable. I know it would be great to receive flowers at work and that could be why he wants to know your work address. Until you know him very well I suggest purchasing your own flowers.

3) The Internet is littered with scam artists

There are several ways you can avoid being a victim of these people. Do not give out personal information until you feel comfortable. Make sure you create an email address that doesn't include your name.

For example: Joannesmith@hotmail.com is not a good email address to use if that's your actual name. Having your name in your email address is good for your resume, not for online dating. Someone may be able to locate you by your name and what part of town you live in.

You Don't Want People To Have Your Personal Information Until You're Ready To Give It To Them.

Yahoo, Gmail, and Hotmail are just three examples of the email platforms that allow you to create an email address for free. Be sure to create an email address that you cannot be identified by.

Unfortunately, I've made that rookie mistake of contacting a guy from my office. After getting to know him, I decided that I didn't want to date him anymore. He called my place of employment incessantly because I wouldn't return his calls. I never actually gave him my work number, but due to modern technology he was able to retrieve my office number off his caller ID. I learned my lesson the hard way.

Con Artists

With all the positive aspects of modern technology, naturally there are also going to be some negative. The Internet is littered with liars, scam artists, and predators and no one ever wants to believe they could fall victim. It's neither pleasant nor comforting to acknowledge the existence of those individuals whom don't have your best interests at heart. The harsh reality is there are a lot of people waiting in line to con you. Joining the world of Internet dating increases your odds of con-artist exposure tenfold. You can meet a con artist anywhere. The Internet allows con-artists to attack more than one person at the same time and it's less risky with cyber-anonymity. These helpful hints will teach you to be cautious and aware of these people.

1) **Never give out your user name or password to any accounts.**

   There is no earthly reason why anyone would need this information from you no matter what line they feed you. Be suspicious of anyone who asks for it.

2) **Never give out your home address.**

   It's ok to give a general area of where you live such as what side of town. There is no reason to give out your address until you are comfortable with them. Again, if someone asks you for your address or even specific locale information, be very suspicious. I believe both men and woman should put this into practice. (Unless he's actually avoiding divulging personal information because he's married, then that's another set up)

3) **Make all your calls on a cell phone.**

   Using your cell phone can be safer than a home phone. It's not a perfect solution, it's only safer. You don't want to run the risk of someone putting your number in a reverse telephone search and getting your address.

4) **Never share where you work.**

You do not want anyone knowing where you work until you feel comfortable. It's ok to let them know your occupation, but employment location is unnecessary information. You also don't want to invite any drama to your work place.

5) **Never give anyone any money.**

This is the single most important hint. If someone ever asks you for money online you should be highly suspicious. If you want to give out money give it to charity. Someone you just met asking for money is not someone you need to be dealing with. You should also be suspicious of people offering to give you money. A common Internet scam is to offer you a monetary gift for whatever reason. Here's the catch, the scammer needs your bank account information to wire the funds. Don't fall prey to this obvious tactic to skim your bank accounts. Some con artists will attempt to use declarations of love and marriage to get in your pockets. Money should not be a requirement for a man to date you. They will try and make you feel bad for not helping them. Never allow someone to use guilt or your desire to be in a relationship to extort money from you.

There's an online scam that's been around for years. A guy posts pictures of a very attractive person. The man in the picture may or may not be the person behind the ads. For all I know it could be a woman performing the scam. He talks to you for a while and then he feeds you a story about having to leave the country in a hurry because of a sick relative. He told me his mother was ill. Then he started to talk about how much he liked me and that he's looking to get married. That's when he went in for the kill. He told me he needed to get back to the United States so he could be with me, but he left so abruptly to tend to his sick mom and he left his money and banking information at home. Since he is looking to marry me and come back to the U.S., I shouldn't have any problem financially assisting him and my reward would be his return to the country to marry me. My assistance was nonexistent because from the beginning of the conversation I knew it was a scam.

Internet Scammers Are The Lowest Life Form On The Planet.

First of all I'm not a fan of anyone asking me for money, especially someone on the other end of a computer. Secondly, I detest people that prey on other people's weaknesses. It's no big mystery that there are a lot of lonely women in the world. If that's you, this book can help you open the door to meet someone that could help you with that issue. The worst feeling is to have someone take advantage of your innate desire for companionship. You have to start using your gut feelings every time you meet someone new. If something doesn't feel right don't continue with the dialogue.

Last year, I went on a dinner date with a very attractive man. After knowing him a week he offered to pay off my credit card debt. I found his offer very suspicious. Why would someone who's only known me a week want to do such a thing? We had only gone out on one date. I asked him flat out, why would you want to pay off my bills? He gave me a lame answer about liking me so much that he didn't want me to stress out over my debts. I told him thanks, but no thanks. That answer was not acceptable to him and he kept pressing the issues. He wanted me to call my credit card company with him on the phone so he could pay them off. I knew he was a con artist so I asked him to write me a check. He of course wasn't going to do that. Then he pushed the issue again. That whole scenario didn't feel right at all. From the very beginning I knew something was off. I decided to do some Internet research on him. I put his full name in a search engine and found a web-site created by a woman he had conned. She even had his mug shot on the page. The page explained he regularly conned women out of money. She also stated that he went into women's homes and took things. Even if I hadn't found that web-page, I still would have not contacted him again because my gut feelings made me suspicious.

Con artists of his caliber prey on women's emotions. They want someone so desperate for male attention they are willing to do anything.

The average man looking to con women are the ones that have nothing to offer you. These men are willing to take as much from you as they can. These people are your typical career unemployed guy who are always looking for work, but never seems to find any. I understand we're in a recession and men and women are getting laid off every day, but I don't understand a man who's willing to live off a woman. I see the same scenario so often and I wonder to myself, what do these women gain from these situations? I'm not referring to the couple that decided that the man should stay home with the children. I'm talking about those women who allow grown men to live in their homes and not contribute anything financially to their households.

I know a woman who was a member of a Christian dating site. She met a man who said he was a preacher. He didn't live in her state, and when he came for a visit he never left. He didn't have a job and she later found out he hadn't worked in years. He had perfected his con and successfully jumped from woman to woman with the same sob story and game for years.

If A Man Is Not An ASSET,
Then He's A LIABILITY.

If he's taking and not giving then he's not worth your time. This is in regards to either monetarily or emotionally using you up. You want a partner not a child you have to take care of.

The moral of the story is be very aware of who you're dealing with and don't just settle for an answer if it doesn't sit right with you. Learn to ask the same question in a different manner. Actively listen and be very observant during your conversations. This will help you sift out the liars. There's a major difference between liars and con artists. Liars never seem to remember their stories. Con artist gives you information on a need to know basis. Trust your instincts if it doesn't sound right it probably isn't, and it's best to move on. Always remember to ask questions about information that can be found on their profile. You'll be shocked to find men will say that they don't have children in their ad profile. Then you talk to them and find out they have three. Some ads will say divorced and when you converse with them further, you'll find out the divorce isn't even final (and in some cases hasn't even been filed). Don't be afraid to ask questions. The only way to know the answer to a question is to ask it. When meeting strangers you have to be aware that not all people have good intentions. There are a lot of people out there taking advantage of women. You don't want to be one of those women. As stated earlier, if you've invested time and energy in him and you feel something isn't right but you are still interested, then get online and use the computer to investigate your suspicions.

The Process

1) Find a dating site that is right for you.

> *There's a plethora of dating sites available on the Internet. There are some that focus on religious beliefs, fetishes, body type, and activities. The key is finding the right site that coincides with your interests.*

2) Decide what you want to accomplish on this site.

> *Whether you're looking for a husband, a friend, or an activity partner, or just someone to talk to, know what you want. Knowing what you want will help when writing your profile. If you're looking for a husband it's always a good rule of thumb to start out as friends first. You*

don't want to come across as too desperate to get married. Most websites are user friendly and have options for you to select. They will list the type of relationship you are looking for such as serious or casual.

3) Once a connection is made go as slow or as fast as you feel comfortable.

Your comfort level is the most important aspect of online dating. If you want to start off slow and email someone and eventually progress to telephone contact that's fine. If you feel comfortable enough to meet after only talking once, that's fine as well. Do what you feel is right for you. Don't let anyone push you out of your comfort zone and don't allow your friends to deter you from putting your best efforts into finding a mate.

4) Meet in a public place.

This requirement is for your personal safety. Until you are comfortable with someone and know who you're dealing with meet in crowded public establishments. Body language says a lot about a person. Always take your time getting to know them.

5) Don't come across as desperate or too needy.

If you're interested in him let it flow naturally. Allow him the opportunity to show you how much he's interested in you. There are men online looking for serious relationships. Let him set the pace. Do not push him in anyway. You can state what you desire. Such as if I find the right person I would love to be married. You just stated what you desired in casual conversation. He could want the same thing and put things on the fast track to see if you will be his future wife, or he could take it slow with no interest in getting married. Let him set the pace. If his pace isn't working for you and time has been invested say what you want. If he is not on the same page move on.

6) Drop him if necessary.

If he's not the right man for you let it go. Don't get caught up in something you don't want. There are plenty more fish in the sea. Never waste your time trying to figure out if he's the right one. If you find yourself asking whether he's right for you more than two times when you first meet someone, then chances are he's not the right one. Move on.

7) **Do not have expectations.**

Do not go into any situation with expectations. If you meet someone online this is a new person. Some relationships can be built on the conversation with wonderful results. Others can be instantly over after you meet this person. He could be totally different than what you envisioned him to be. His communication and mannerisms in person could be a deal breaker or the icing on the cake. I've been on several dates when I knew immediately after spending time with him it wasn't going to work. For example, I met a man whose pictures were gorgeous and his conversation intrigued me over the course of several days. The date ruined everything. We met at a restaurant and he arrived unshaven, needing a haircut, and his clothes looked like he should have thrown them out years ago. Everything seemed perfect until we met. His appearance in person was a total deal breaker for me.

Conclusion

Now that you've learned the basic tricks of the trade we've reached the end of our journey and it's time to put your plan into action. Go get yourself pampered, let your hair down, take some smoking hot pictures, and get started. The man for you might be a few clicks a way. You'll never know until you try. There's nothing wrong with starting out as a more casual Internet dater by posting a profile to see what comes your way. If you want to you may also take the more aggressive route and email all the men you're interested in. Stop spending your time alone and make it happen! Remember never lower your standards, but make sure those standards aren't unrealistic.

If nothing else enjoy a few dates and stop spending Friday nights in front of the TV. Replace your singleton lifestyle that you've grown accustomed to and explore the net for a possible future mate to share your life with.

There are many dating sites that could be for you. I've even given you a jump start on your web search by providing some of the more popular dating sites in an appendix. If you don't see one that piques your interest, simply go to your search engine and look for the site that best suits your needs.

So Remember Be Classy, Be Confident, Be Careful and Have Fun!

Appendix: Web-Site Directory

Popular

www.match.com

www.eharmony.com

www.personals.yahoo.com

www.chemistry.com

www.perfectmatch.com

www.lavalife.com

Special Interest

www.tangowire.com

www.fling.com

www.singleparentmingle.com

www.bbwmatcher.com

www.moretolove.com

www.sugardaddie.com

www.wealthymen.com

www.ashleymadison.com

www.adultfriendfinder.com

www.romanceopedia.com

www.seniorpeoplemeet.com

www.maturedatelink.com

www.positivesingles.com

Free

www.craigslist.com

www.plentyoffish.com

www.tagged.com

Race

www.blackpeoplemeet.com

www.asiansinglesconnection.com

www.italiansinglesconnection.com

www.blacksinglesconnection.com

www.minglecity.com

www.migente.com

www.interracialdatingcentral.com

www.afroromance.com

Religion

www.catholicmingle.com

www.catholicmatch.com

www.jdate.com

www.blackfaithlove.com

Social Networking

www.facebook.com

www.myspace.com

www.blackplanet.com

www.twitter.com

Finding Background Information

www.intelius.com

www.backgroundchecks.com

www.zabasearch.com

www.dontdatehimgirl.com

www.peoplelookup.com